P.S.
I LOVE YOU

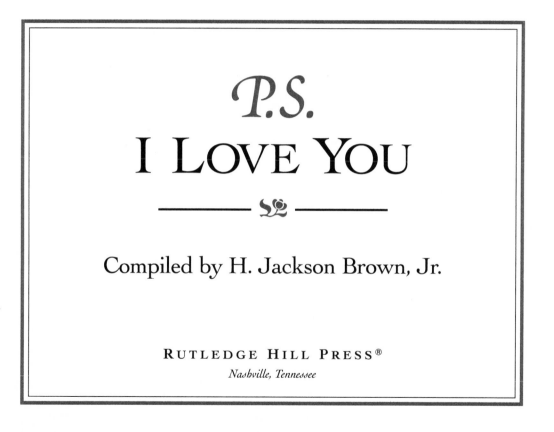

Compiled by H. Jackson Brown, Jr.

RUTLEDGE HILL PRESS®

Nashville, Tennessee

Published in Nashville, Tennessee, by Rutledge Hill Press, Inc., 211 Seventh Avenue North, Nashville, Tennessee 37219.

Distributed in Canada by H. B. Fenn & Company, Ltd., 34 Nixon Road, Bolton, Ontario, L7E 1W2. Distributed in Australia by The Five Mile Press Pty., Ltd., 22 Summit Road, Noble Park, Victoria 3174. Distributed in New Zealand by Tandem Press, 2 Rugby Road, Birkenhead, Auckland 10. Distributed in the United Kingdom by Verulam Publishing, Ltd., 152a Park Street Lane, Park Street, St. Albans, Hertfordshire AL2 2AU.

Design by Bruce Gore/Gore Studio, Inc.

Library of Congress Cataloging-in-Publication Data

P.S. I Love You

1. Letter writing—Humor. 2. Mothers—Humor.
I. Brown, H. Jackson, 1940-   II. Title: PS I love you
PN6231.L44P25   1990   816'.54   90-8309
ISBN 1-55853-753-8

Manufactured in the United States of America

 2 3 4 5 6 7 8 9 — 03 02 01 00 99

INTRODUCTION

Over the years Mom has written my sister and me hundreds of letters. What we cherished most were the little P.S. notes she would write at the end of each one. There, in just a few words, she would encourage and inspire us with keen observations, gentle humor, and loving advice.

We saved the letters, and this little book is a collection of her P.S. messages we love the most. Although some were written more than forty years ago, they still ring with truth and insight.

I hope you will enjoy reading them. Perhaps you will be reminded of similar words of wisdom written to you by your mother or father.

As I write this, I am happy to report that Mom is in excellent health and still writing. I can't wait for her next letter.

H. J. B.

Dedicated to my mother whose love, laughter, encouragement, and values will always guide and inspire me.

Thanks, Mom. I love you.

H. J. B.

OTHER BOOKS BY H. JACKSON BROWN, JR.

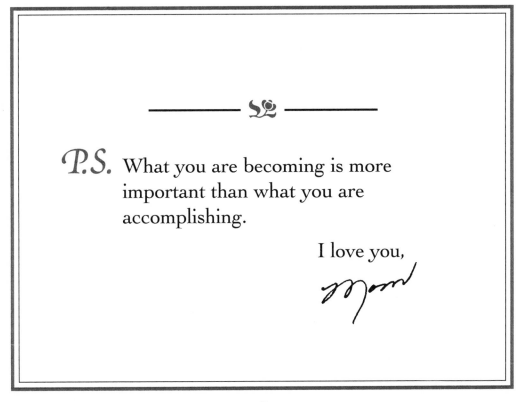

P.S. What you are becoming is more important than what you are accomplishing.

I love you,

Mom

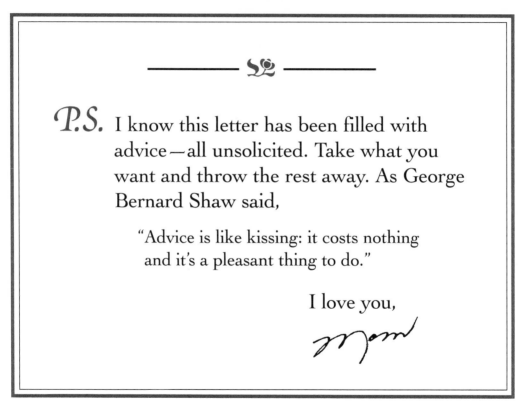

P.S. I know this letter has been filled with advice—all unsolicited. Take what you want and throw the rest away. As George Bernard Shaw said,

> "Advice is like kissing: it costs nothing and it's a pleasant thing to do."

I love you,

Mom

P.S. I love this story about giving credit where credit is due:

> A preacher comes up to a farmer in his field and remarks, "Mighty fine farm you and the Lord have made." "Yep," replies the farmer, "but you should have seen it when He had it all to Himself."

I love you,

Mom

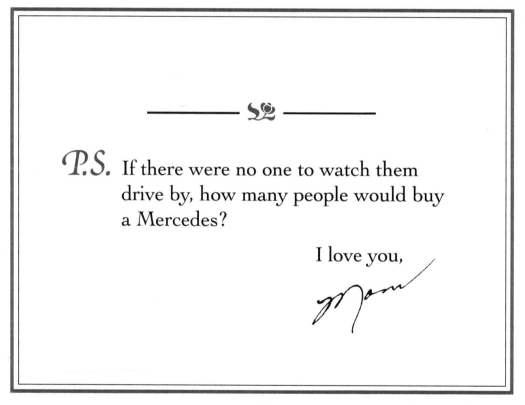

P.S. If there were no one to watch them drive by, how many people would buy a Mercedes?

I love you,

Mom

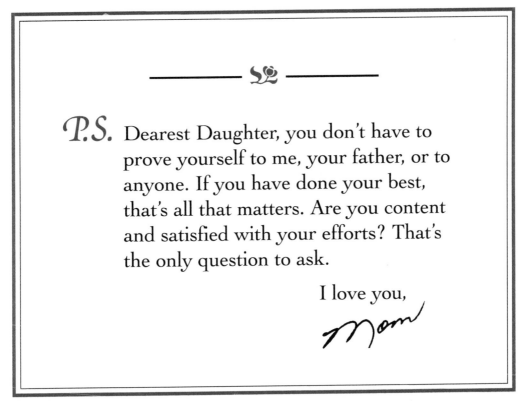

P.S. Dearest Daughter, you don't have to prove yourself to me, your father, or to anyone. If you have done your best, that's all that matters. Are you content and satisfied with your efforts? That's the only question to ask.

I love you,

Mom

P.S. Regarding your D in biology, let me only say that sometimes a good scare is worth more than good advice.

I love you,

Mom

P.S. One of your father's clients sent him a lovely paperweight with this inscription:

> People can be divided into three groups:
> Those who make things happen
> Those who watch things happen
> Those who wonder what happened
> Congratulations on being the captain of the first group.

You have a very special father.

I love you,

Mom

P.S. You're learning that nothing worthwhile ever comes without hard work. As Grandfather Harper used to say,

"To enjoy the cider you must first peel the apple."

I love you,

Mom

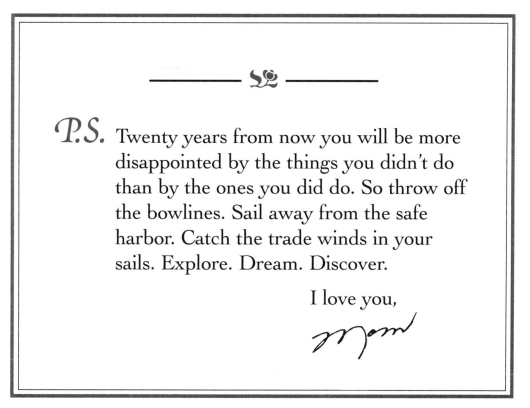

P.S. Twenty years from now you will be more disappointed by the things you didn't do than by the ones you did do. So throw off the bowlines. Sail away from the safe harbor. Catch the trade winds in your sails. Explore. Dream. Discover.

I love you,

Mom

P.S. An older gentleman in front of me at the check-out at Kroger's was wearing a hat with this inscription:

IF WE HAD KNOWN GRANDKIDS WERE SO MUCH FUN, WE'D HAVE HAD THEM FIRST.

I bet he's a great granddad!

I love you,

Mom

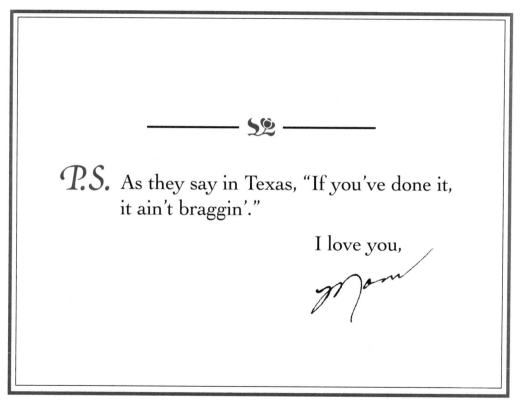

P.S. As they say in Texas, "If you've done it, it ain't braggin'."

I love you,

Mom

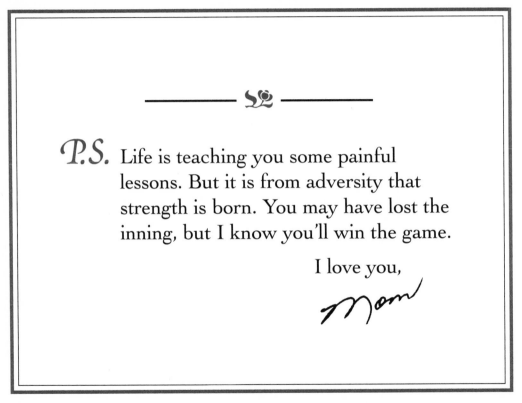

P.S. Life is teaching you some painful
lessons. But it is from adversity that
strength is born. You may have lost the
inning, but I know you'll win the game.

I love you,

Mom

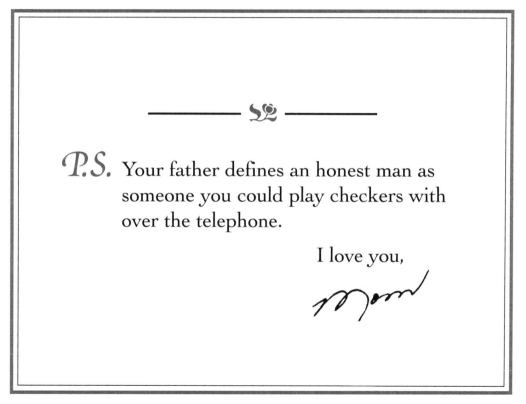

P.S. Your father defines an honest man as someone you could play checkers with over the telephone.

I love you,

Mom

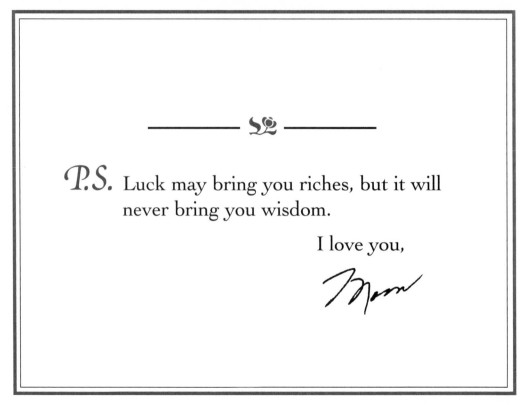

P.S. Luck may bring you riches, but it will never bring you wisdom.

I love you,

Mom

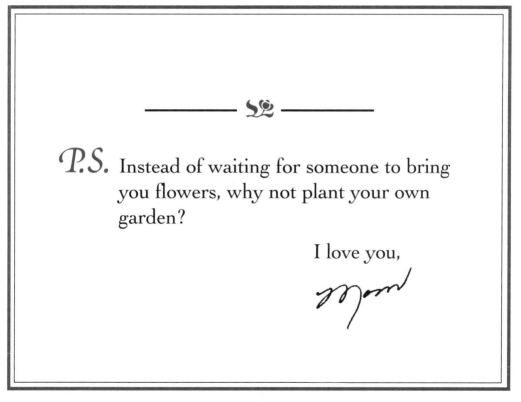

P.S. Instead of waiting for someone to bring you flowers, why not plant your own garden?

I love you,

Mom

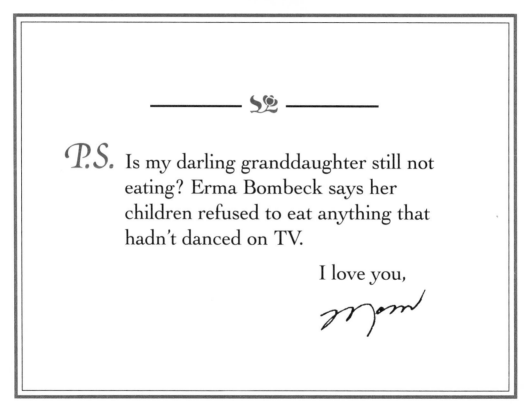

P.S. Is my darling granddaughter still not eating? Erma Bombeck says her children refused to eat anything that hadn't danced on TV.

I love you,

Mom

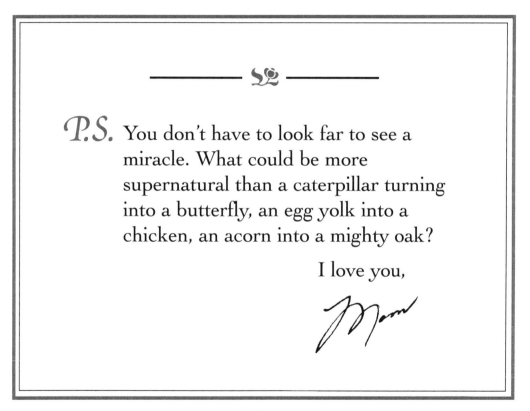

P.S. You don't have to look far to see a miracle. What could be more supernatural than a caterpillar turning into a butterfly, an egg yolk into a chicken, an acorn into a mighty oak?

I love you,

Mom

P.S. Last week I met a young salesman in a shoe store wearing this button:

He'd made it himself. I love it!

I love you,

Mom

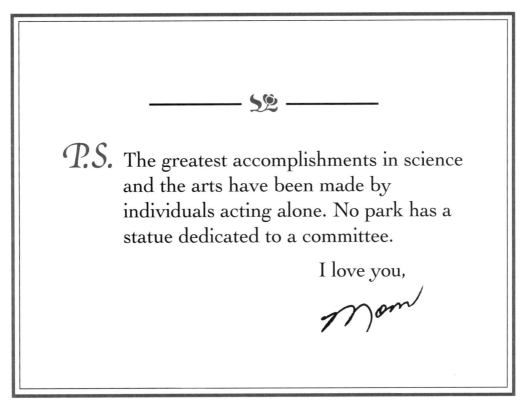

P.S. The greatest accomplishments in science and the arts have been made by individuals acting alone. No park has a statue dedicated to a committee.

I love you,

Mom

P.S. You'll never build a reputation, a business, or a relationship on what you *intend* to do. Your intentions may be honorable and sincere, but unless you put them into action, nothing is changed.

I love you,

Mom

———— 🌹 ————

P.S. No failure is ever final—nor is any success.

I love you,

Mom

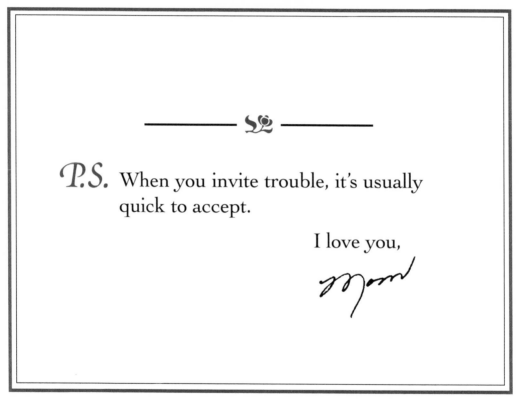

P.S. When you invite trouble, it's usually quick to accept.

I love you,

Mom

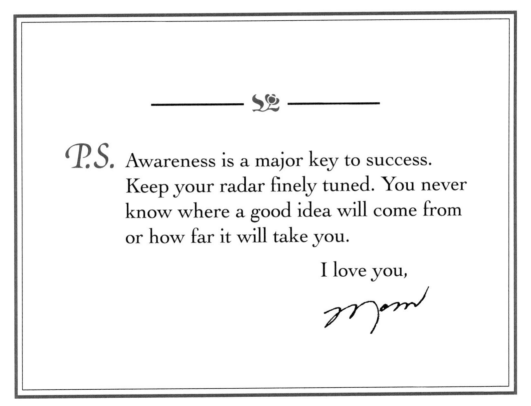

P.S. Awareness is a major key to success. Keep your radar finely tuned. You never know where a good idea will come from or how far it will take you.

I love you,

Mom

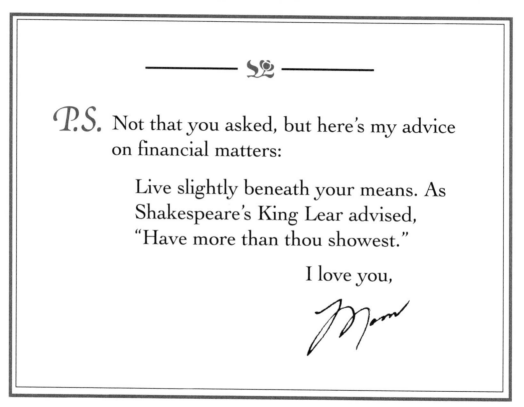

P.S. Not that you asked, but here's my advice on financial matters:

Live slightly beneath your means. As Shakespeare's King Lear advised, "Have more than thou showest."

I love you,

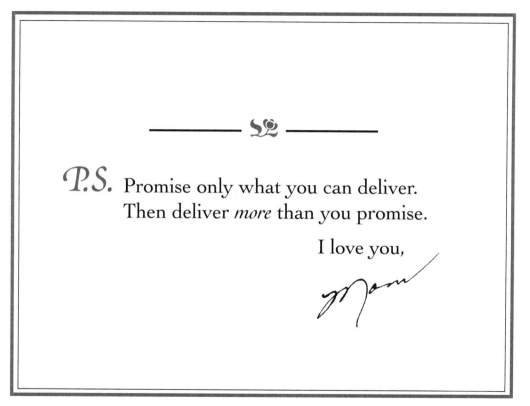

P.S. Promise only what you can deliver.
Then deliver *more* than you promise.

I love you,

Mom

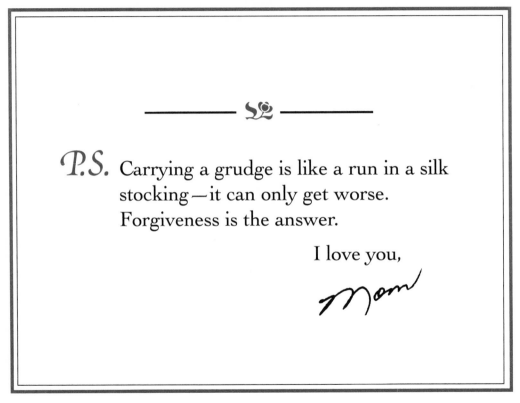

P.S. Carrying a grudge is like a run in a silk stocking—it can only get worse. Forgiveness is the answer.

I love you,

Mom

———————— ❧ ————————

P.S. Dale Carnegie wrote this almost fifty years ago. It's as true today as it was then:

> "You can make more friends in two months by becoming genuinely interested in other people than you can in two years by trying to get other people interested in you."

I love you,

Mom

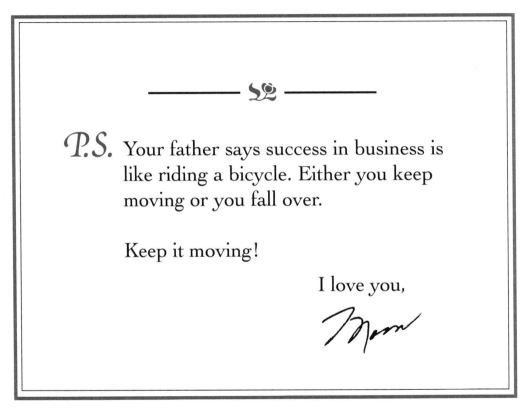

P.S. Your father says success in business is like riding a bicycle. Either you keep moving or you fall over.

Keep it moving!

I love you,

Mom

P.S. The only thing that ever sat its way to success was a hen.

I love you,

Mom

CLUCK! CLUCK!

P.S. A survey asked, "Who are the happiest people?" The four winning answers were:

A craftsman or artist whistling over a job well done.

A child building sand castles.

A mother bathing her baby.

A doctor who has finished a difficult operation and saved a life.

Money, power, and possessions were not mentioned.

I love you,

Mom

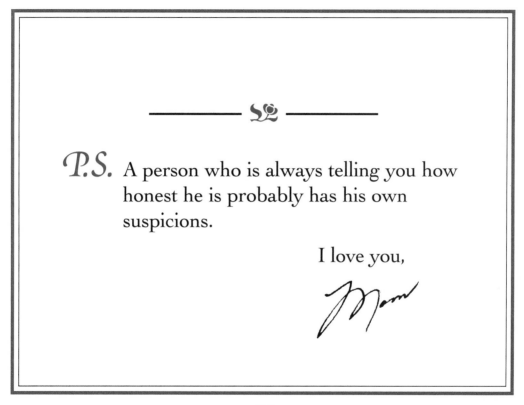

P.S. A person who is always telling you how honest he is probably has his own suspicions.

I love you,

Mom

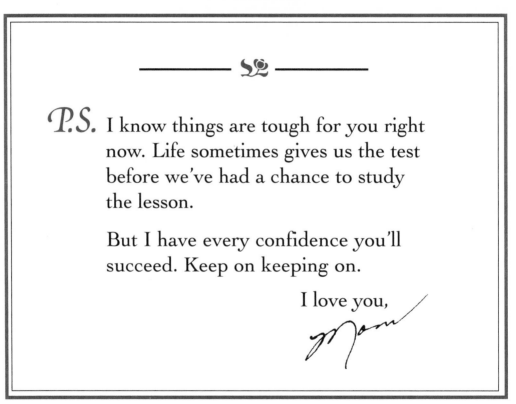

P.S. I know things are tough for you right now. Life sometimes gives us the test before we've had a chance to study the lesson.

But I have every confidence you'll succeed. Keep on keeping on.

I love you,

Mom

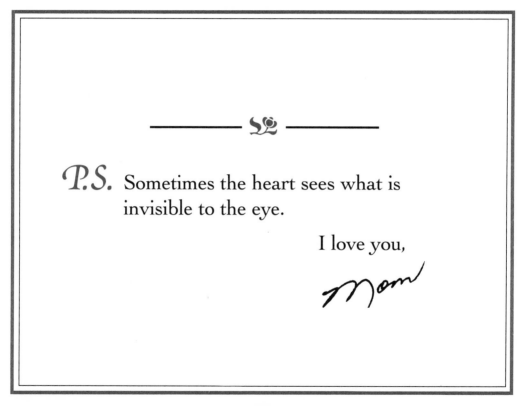

P.S. Sometimes the heart sees what is invisible to the eye.

I love you,

Mom

P.S. Your father just finished Paul "Bear" Bryant's book. Here's what he writes about motivating others:

> "If anything goes bad, I did it.
> If anything goes semi-good, we did it.
> If anything goes real good, then you did it.
> That's all it takes to get people to win
> football games for you."

This works wonders in the game of life, too.

I love you,

Mom

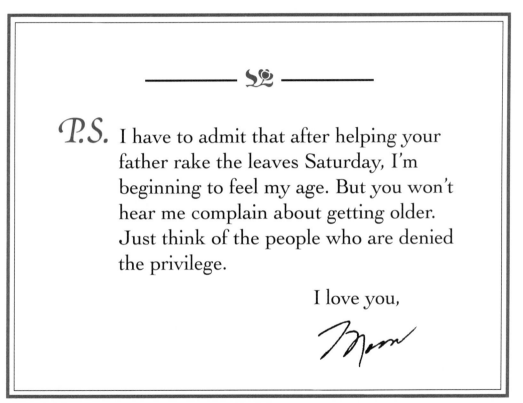

P.S. I have to admit that after helping your father rake the leaves Saturday, I'm beginning to feel my age. But you won't hear me complain about getting older. Just think of the people who are denied the privilege.

I love you,

Mom

P.S. I saw a sign with the word **FIDO** in the back window of a Winnebago at a filling station. I asked the driver if it was the name of his dog. "Oh no," he replied. "It's just a reminder that when someone is discourteous to me on the road I should just **F**orget **I**t and **D**rive **O**n."

Good advice.

I love you,

Mom

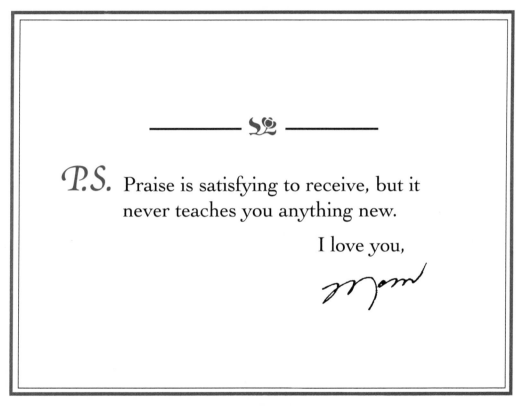

P.S. Praise is satisfying to receive, but it never teaches you anything new.

I love you,

Mom

--- ❧ ---

P.S. Do for others with no desire of returned favors. We all should plant some trees we'll never sit under.

I love you,

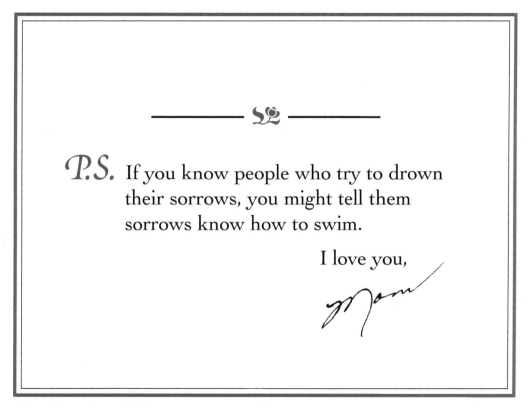

P.S. If you know people who try to drown their sorrows, you might tell them sorrows know how to swim.

I love you,

Mom

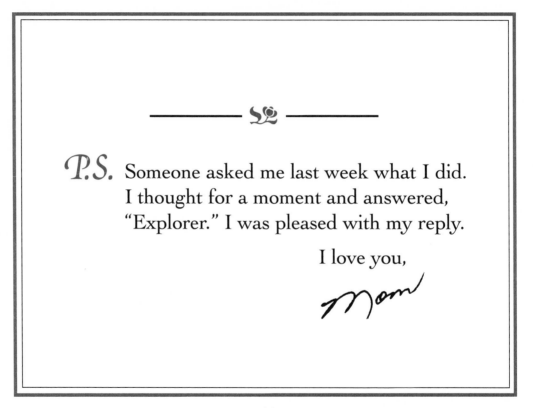

P.S. Someone asked me last week what I did. I thought for a moment and answered, "Explorer." I was pleased with my reply.

I love you,

Mom

P.S. Don't be afraid to go out on a limb.
That's where the fruit is.

I love you,

Mom

---- ✿ ----

P.S. Here's my favorite bumper sticker that we saw on our trip to St. Louis:

IF YOU'RE HEADED IN
THE WRONG DIRECTION,
GOD ALLOWS **U-TURNS.**

I love you,

Mom

P.S. Now that you and your sister are graduated, happily married, and working at jobs that are challenging and financially rewarding, your father and I feel it's finally our time. Someone said, "Life doesn't begin at conception, nor at birth, but when the kids leave home and the dog dies." We eagerly await the next chapter in our lives. Wagons ho!

I love you,

Mom

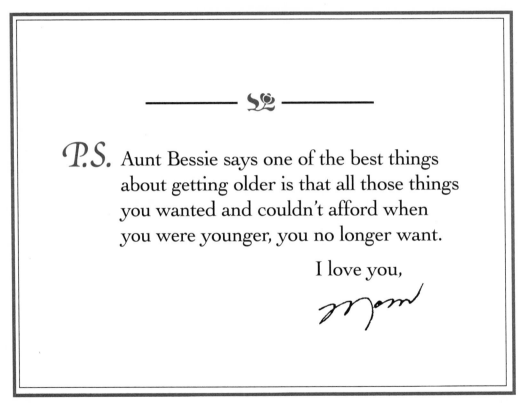

P.S. Aunt Bessie says one of the best things
about getting older is that all those things
you wanted and couldn't afford when
you were younger, you no longer want.

I love you,

Mom

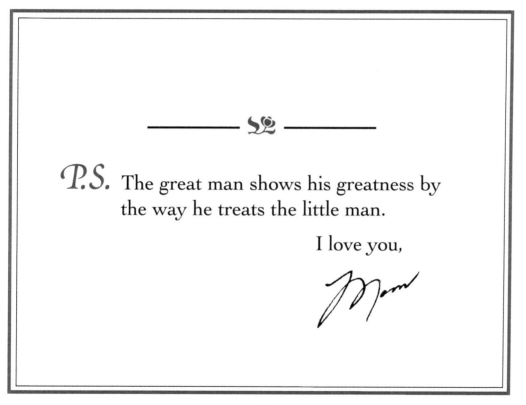

P.S. The great man shows his greatness by
the way he treats the little man.

I love you,

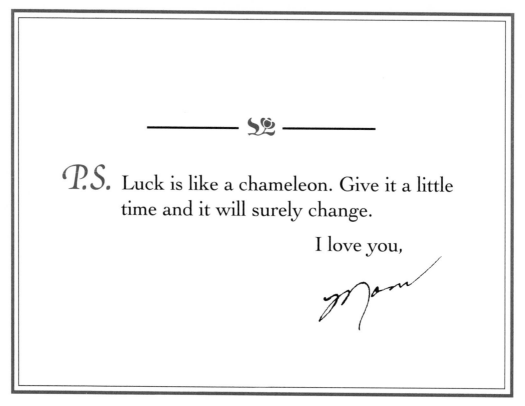

P.S. Luck is like a chameleon. Give it a little time and it will surely change.

I love you,

Mom

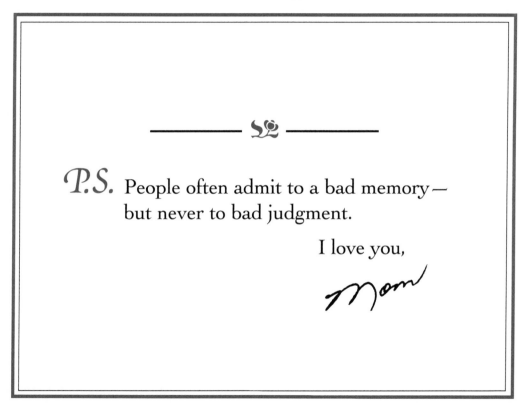

P.S. People often admit to a bad memory—
but never to bad judgment.

I love you,

Mom

P.S. When you are angry or frustrated, what comes out? Whatever it is, it's a good indication of what you're made of.

I love you,

Mom

P.S. I've just finished reading the book *The 100 Most Influential Persons in History*. I am struck by the one thing I have in common with all of them —time. These men and women who changed the world did not have any more hours a day than you and I. I'm convinced judicious use of time is one of the major contributors to success.

I love you,

Mom

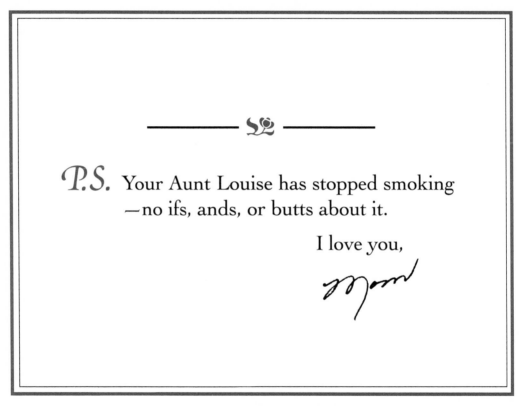

P.S. Your Aunt Louise has stopped smoking —no ifs, ands, or butts about it.

I love you,

Mom

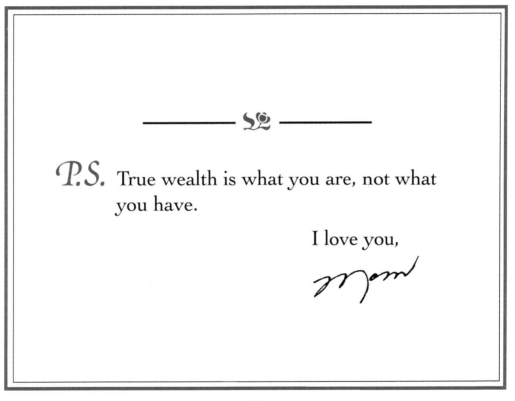

P.S. True wealth is what you are, not what you have.

I love you,

Mom

P.S. We seldom enjoy leisure we haven't earned.

I love you,

Mom

P.S. If at the end of a day you feel dog-tired, maybe it's because you growled all day.

G·R·R·R·R!

I love you,

Mom

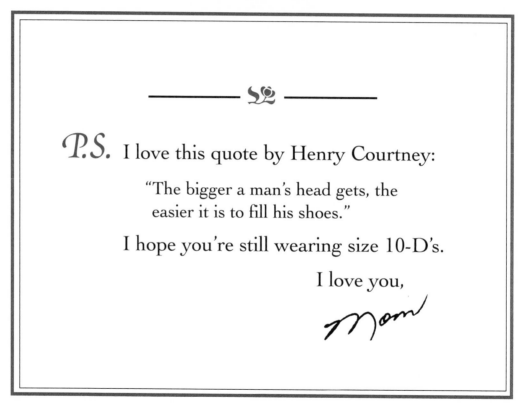

P.S. I love this quote by Henry Courtney:

"The bigger a man's head gets, the easier it is to fill his shoes."

I hope you're still wearing size 10-D's.

I love you,

Mom

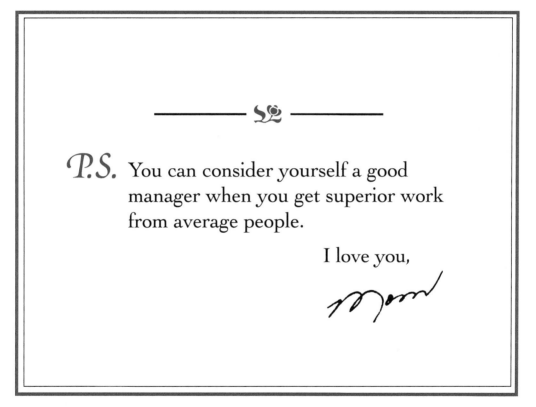

P.S. You can consider yourself a good manager when you get superior work from average people.

I love you,

Mom

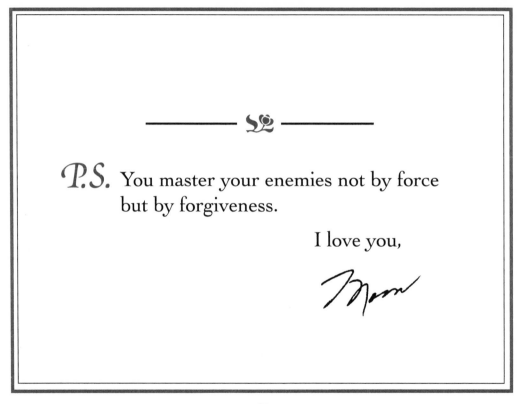

P.S. You master your enemies not by force but by forgiveness.

I love you,

Mom

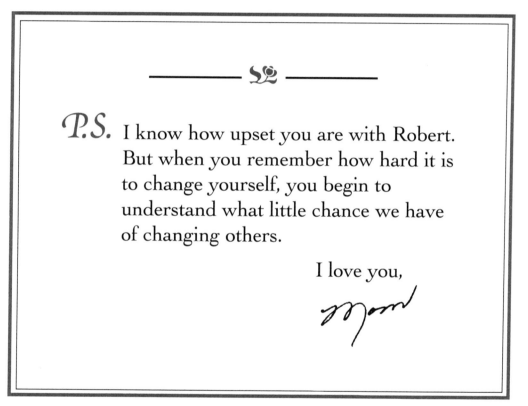

P.S. I know how upset you are with Robert. But when you remember how hard it is to change yourself, you begin to understand what little chance we have of changing others.

I love you,

——— ❧ ———

P.S. Margaret and I have gone on the "see-food" diet. We see food and we eat it.

I love you,

Mom

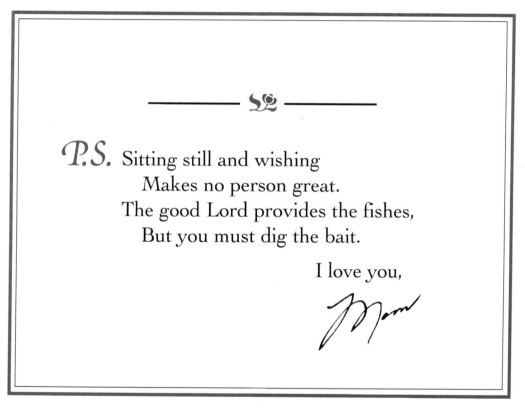

P.S. Sitting still and wishing
        Makes no person great.
The good Lord provides the fishes,
        But you must dig the bait.

I love you,

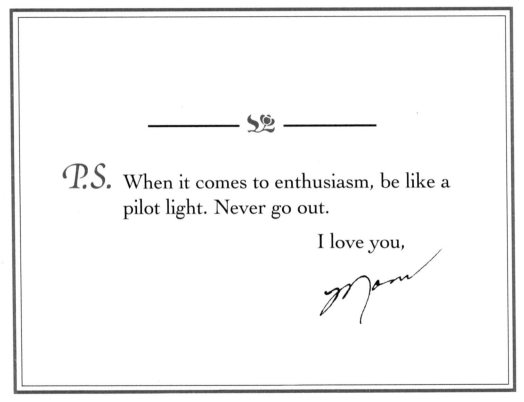

P.S. When it comes to enthusiasm, be like a pilot light. Never go out.

I love you,

Mom

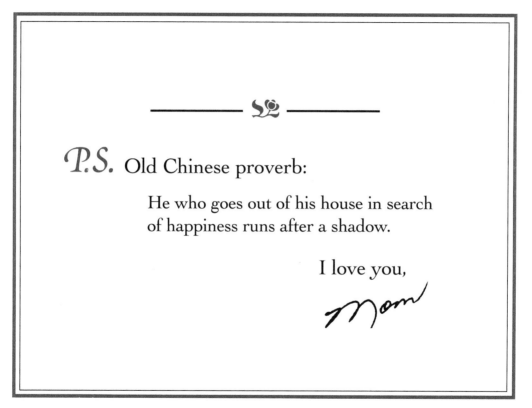

P.S. Old Chinese proverb:

He who goes out of his house in search of happiness runs after a shadow.

I love you,

Mom

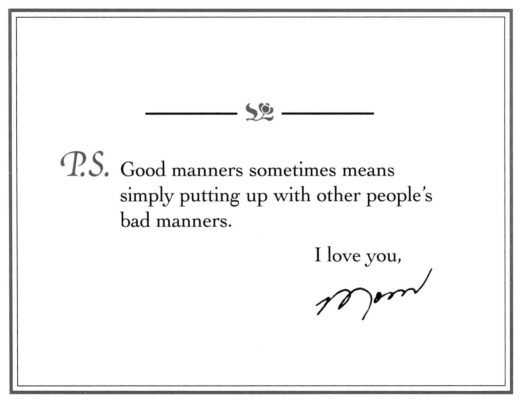

P.S. Good manners sometimes means simply putting up with other people's bad manners.

I love you,

Mom

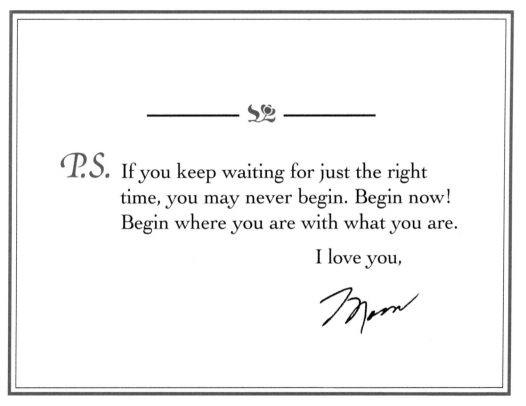

P.S. If you keep waiting for just the right time, you may never begin. Begin now! Begin where you are with what you are.

I love you,

Mom

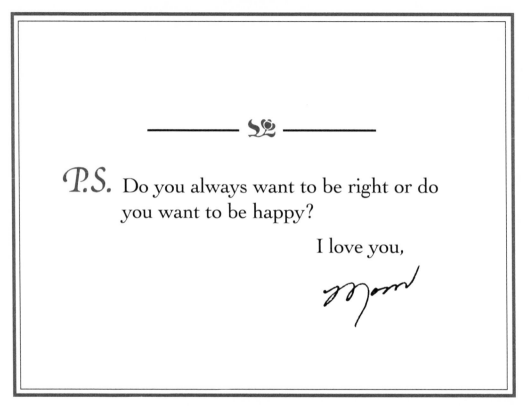

P.S. Do you always want to be right or do
you want to be happy?

I love you,

P.S. Sorry to hear about your first confrontation with a customer. Here's a response that's always worked for me. The next time you face a customer who has every right to be upset say something like this:

"I don't blame you for feeling as you do. If I were you, I'd feel exactly the same way. What would you like for me to do?"

These are magical, healing words and you'll be surprised at how reasonable people become when they feel you are on their side.

I love you,

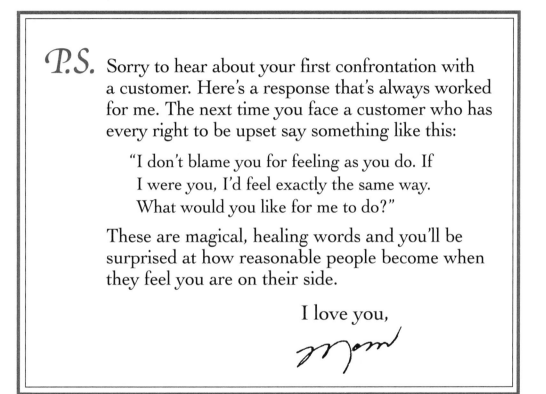

P.S. Regarding the contract with your publisher, read it carefully. Remember, the big print giveth and the small print taketh away.

I love you,

Mom

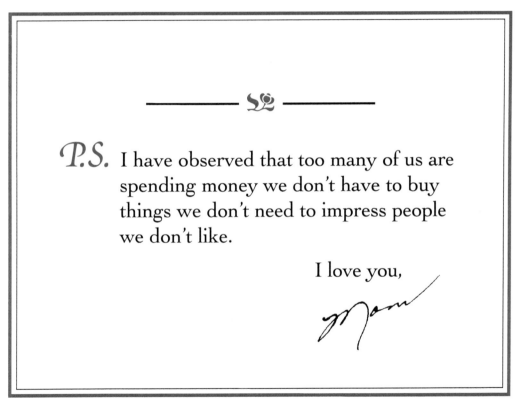

P.S. I have observed that too many of us are spending money we don't have to buy things we don't need to impress people we don't like.

I love you,

Mom

P.S. For Julie's fortieth birthday, someone gave her an enormous card with this inscription:

When you're over
the hill, you
pick up speed.

Your father and I are really cruisin'!

I love you,

Mom

P.S. There's trouble at your father's office. An employee is suing. Your father says you enter a lawsuit a pig and come out a sausage.

Oink.

I love you,

Mom

———— ❧ ————

P.S. When fate shuts a door, come in through the window.

I love you,

Mom

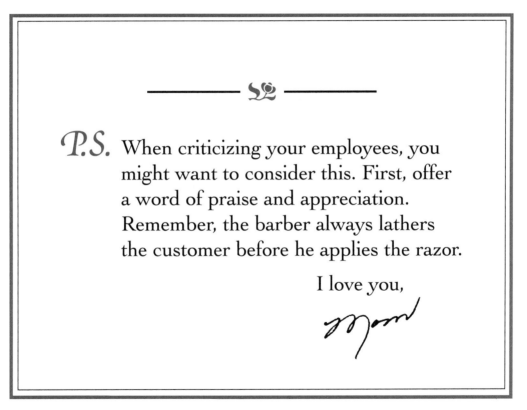

P.S. When criticizing your employees, you might want to consider this. First, offer a word of praise and appreciation. Remember, the barber always lathers the customer before he applies the razor.

I love you,

Mom

P.S. The most important thing a father can do for his children is to love their mother.

Your father does such a good job of this.

I love you,

Mom

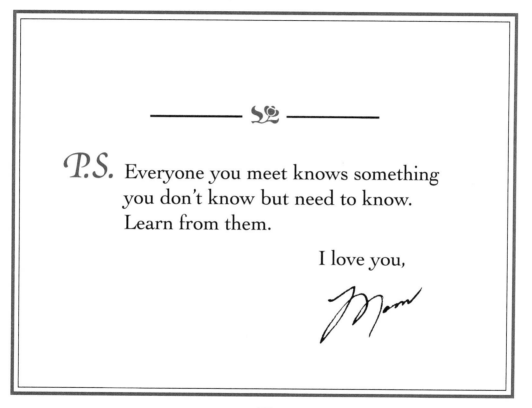

P.S. Everyone you meet knows something
you don't know but need to know.
Learn from them.

I love you,

Mom

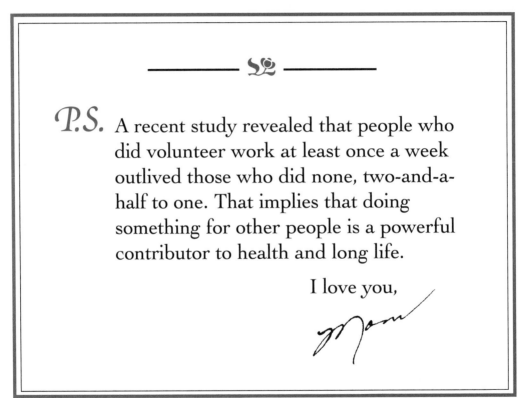

P.S. A recent study revealed that people who did volunteer work at least once a week outlived those who did none, two-and-a-half to one. That implies that doing something for other people is a powerful contributor to health and long life.

I love you,

Mom

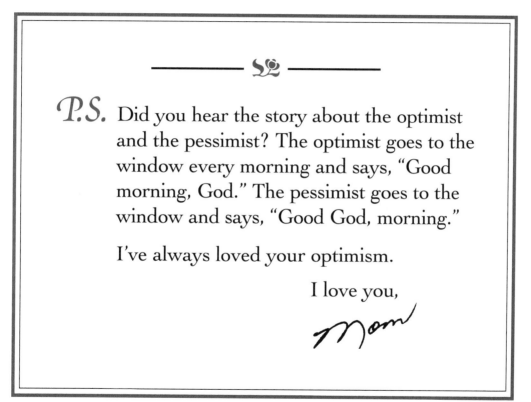

P.S. Did you hear the story about the optimist and the pessimist? The optimist goes to the window every morning and says, "Good morning, God." The pessimist goes to the window and says, "Good God, morning."

I've always loved your optimism.

I love you,

Mom

———— 🌹 ————

P.S. Your father says inflation hasn't ruined everything. A dime can still be used as a screwdriver.

I love you,

Mom

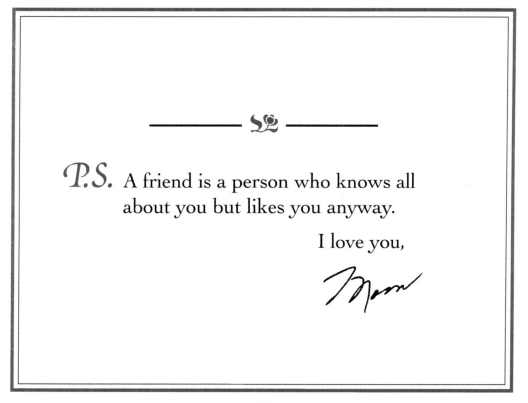

P.S. A friend is a person who knows all about you but likes you anyway.

I love you,

Mom

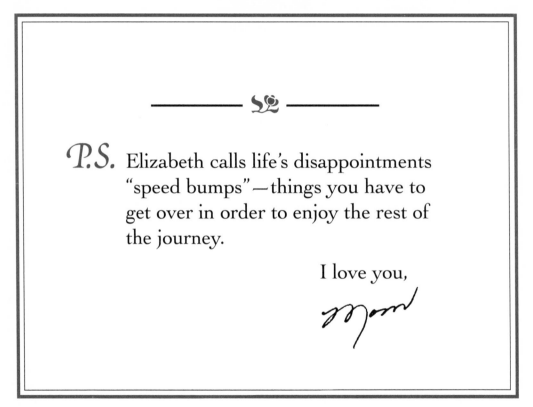

P.S. Elizabeth calls life's disappointments "speed bumps"—things you have to get over in order to enjoy the rest of the journey.

I love you,

Mom

P.S. Uncle Henry says he knows he's getting old because last week thieves broke into his car and stole his cassette deck, but left his tapes.

I love you,

Mom

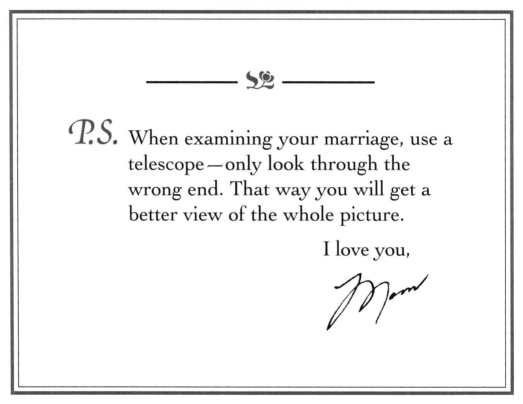

P.S. When examining your marriage, use a telescope—only look through the wrong end. That way you will get a better view of the whole picture.

I love you,

Mom

P.S. You'll learn more about a road by traveling it than by consulting all the maps in the world.

I love you,

Mom

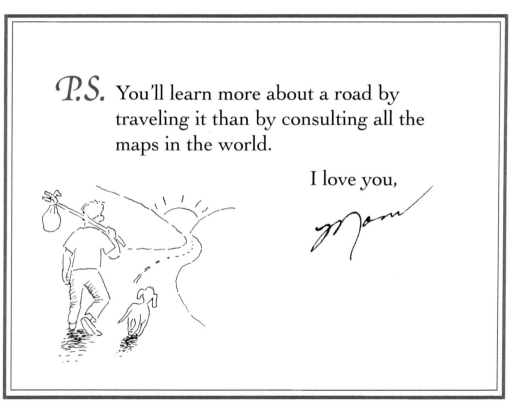

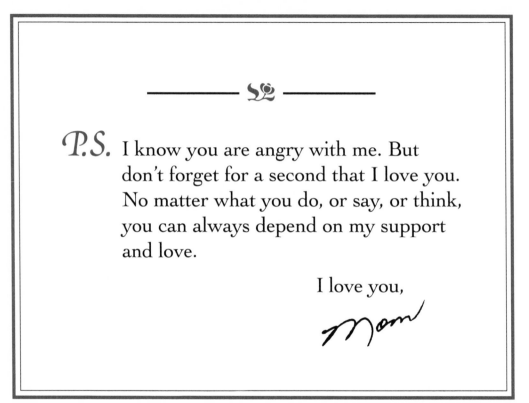

P.S. I know you are angry with me. But don't forget for a second that I love you. No matter what you do, or say, or think, you can always depend on my support and love.

I love you,

Mom

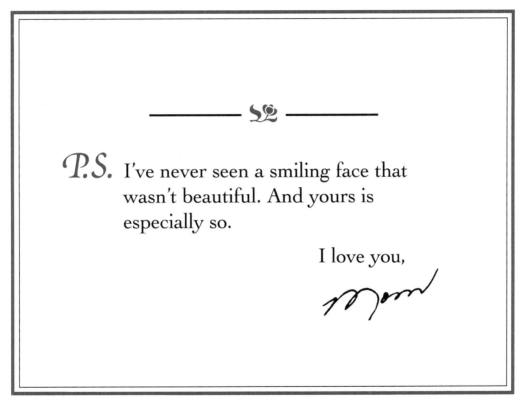

P.S. I've never seen a smiling face that wasn't beautiful. And yours is especially so.

I love you,

Mom

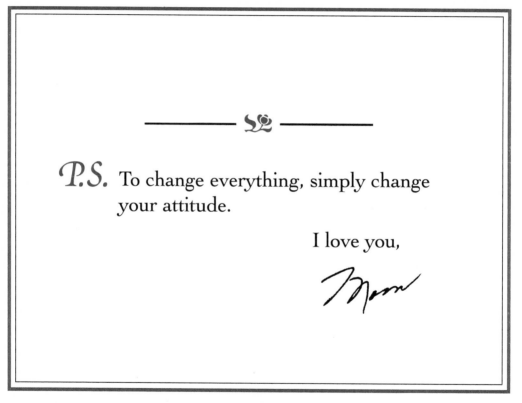

P.S. To change everything, simply change
your attitude.

I love you,

Mom

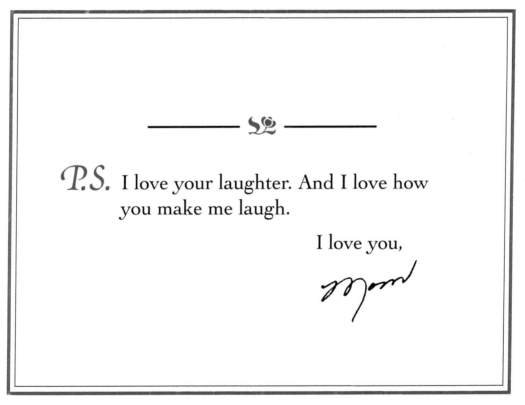

P.S. I love your laughter. And I love how you make me laugh.

I love you,

Mom

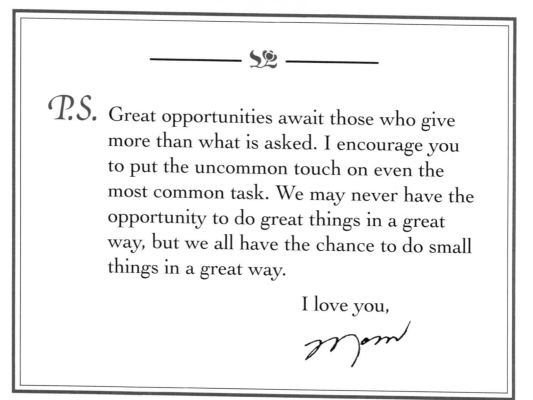

P.S. Great opportunities await those who give more than what is asked. I encourage you to put the uncommon touch on even the most common task. We may never have the opportunity to do great things in a great way, but we all have the chance to do small things in a great way.

I love you,

Mom

--- ❧ ---

P.S. To be bitter is to waste precious moments of a life that's too short already.

I love you,

Mom

P.S. Today, give a stranger one of your smiles. It might be the only sunshine he sees all day.

I love you,

Mom

P.S. Do you want credit or results? This quote hangs in the office of the president of Neiman-Marcus:

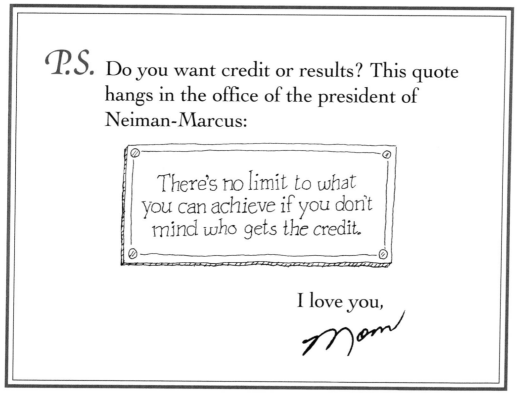

There's no limit to what you can achieve if you don't mind who gets the credit.

I love you,

Mom

P.S. An advertising executive once told his associates:

> "Reach for the stars. You might not get them, but you won't wind up with a handful of mud either."

I love you,

Mom

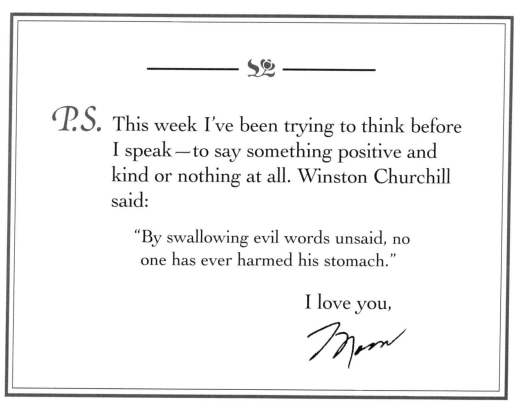

P.S. This week I've been trying to think before I speak—to say something positive and kind or nothing at all. Winston Churchill said:

"By swallowing evil words unsaid, no one has ever harmed his stomach."

I love you,

Mom

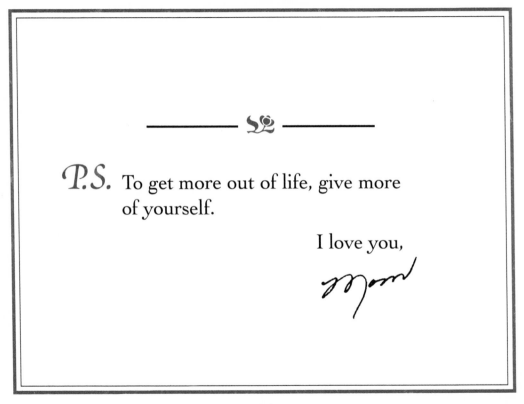

P.S. To get more out of life, give more
of yourself.

I love you,

Mom

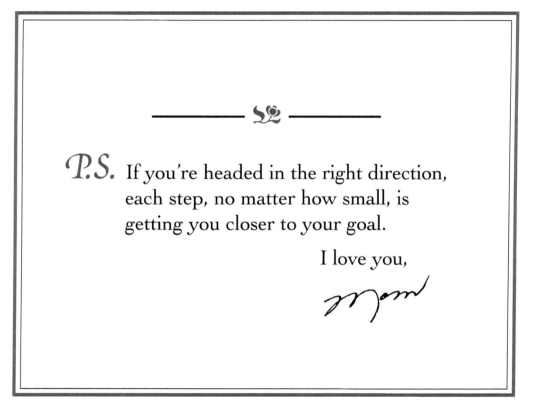

P.S. If you're headed in the right direction, each step, no matter how small, is getting you closer to your goal.

I love you,

Mom

P.S. Go for it! Take a chance. There are times you must trust that silent voice inside you. The experts don't always have the right answers.

According to the laws of aerodynamics the bumble bee cannot fly. I guess no one bothered to tell the bee.

Keep flying!

I love you,

Mom

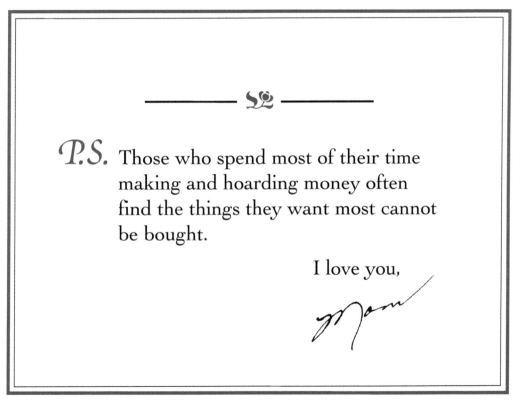

P.S. Those who spend most of their time making and hoarding money often find the things they want most cannot be bought.

I love you,

Mom

———— 🌹 ————

P.S. Dreams come true for those who work while they dream.

Sweet dreams.

I love you,

Mom

P.S. In an interview, the actor Michael Caine told how his mother encouraged him to be like a duck —calm on the surface but always paddling like the dickens underneath.

I love you,

Mom

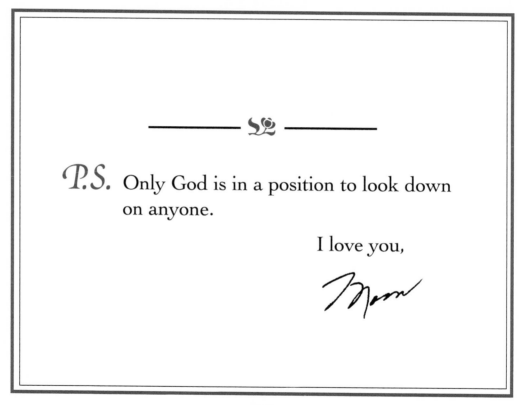

P.S. Only God is in a position to look down on anyone.

I love you,

Mom

P.S. Congratulations on your summer job.
As a new sales associate, just remember
true salesmanship begins when the
customer says "no."

I love you,

Mom

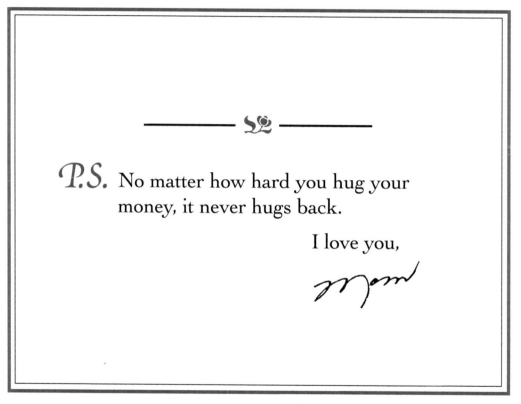

P.S. No matter how hard you hug your money, it never hugs back.

I love you,

Mom

P.S. No one is guaranteed happiness. Life just gives each person time and space. It's up to us to fill it with joy.

I love you,

Mom

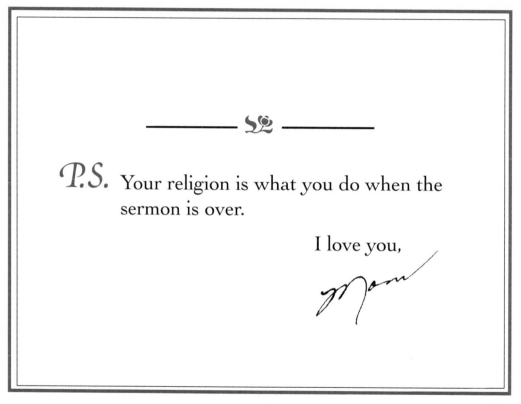

P.S. Your religion is what you do when the sermon is over.

I love you,

Mom

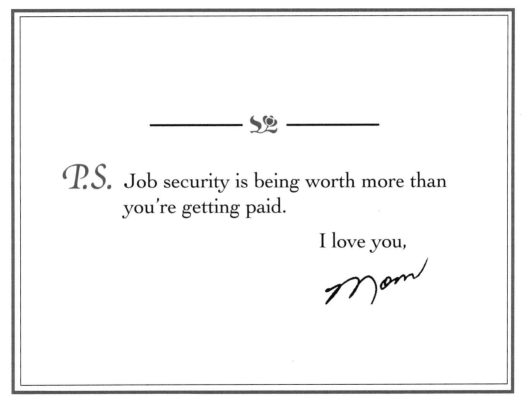

P.S. Job security is being worth more than you're getting paid.

I love you,

Mom

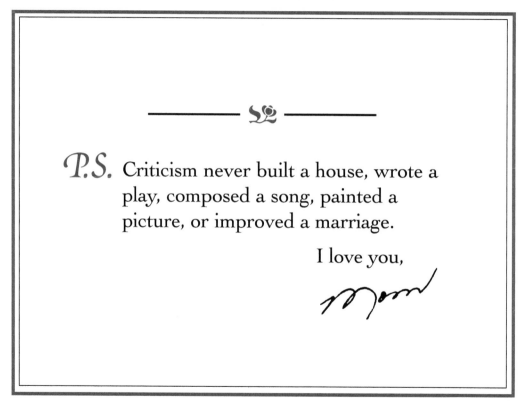

P.S. Criticism never built a house, wrote a play, composed a song, painted a picture, or improved a marriage.

I love you,

Mom

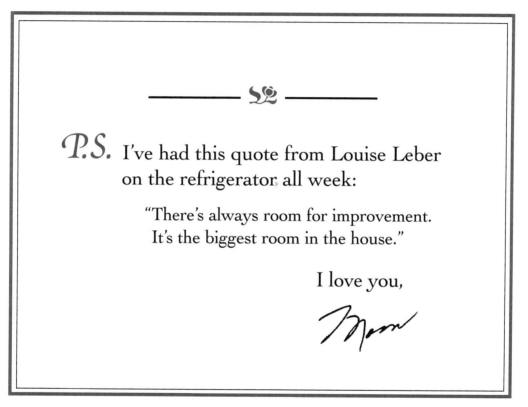

P.S. I've had this quote from Louise Leber on the refrigerator all week:

"There's always room for improvement. It's the biggest room in the house."

I love you,

Mom

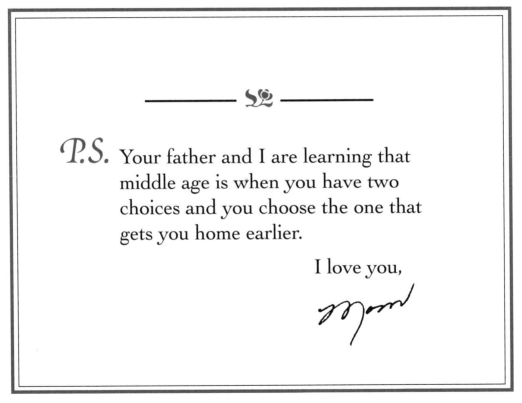

P.S. Your father and I are learning that middle age is when you have two choices and you choose the one that gets you home earlier.

I love you,

Mom

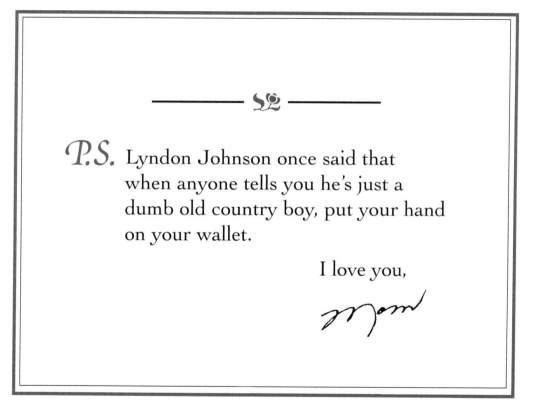

P.S. Lyndon Johnson once said that when anyone tells you he's just a dumb old country boy, put your hand on your wallet.

I love you,

Mom

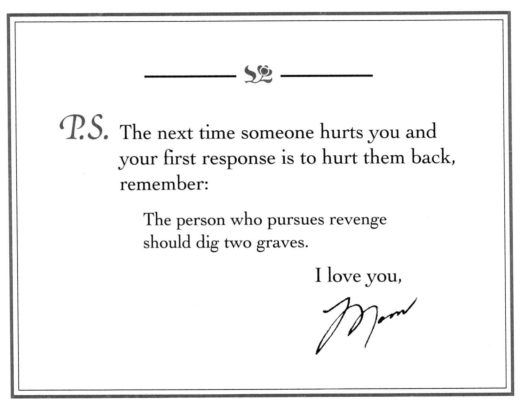

P.S. The next time someone hurts you and your first response is to hurt them back, remember:

The person who pursues revenge should dig two graves.

I love you,

Mom

P.S. A trainee has this sign on his desk at your father's business:

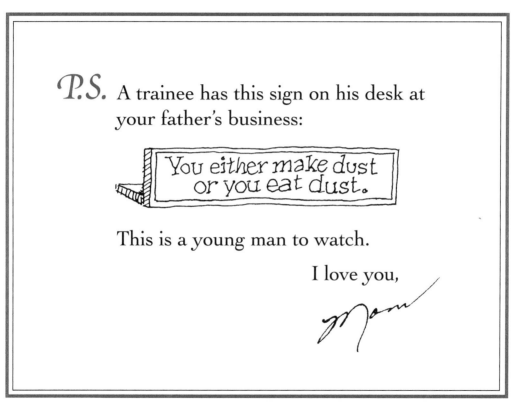

This is a young man to watch.

I love you,

Mom

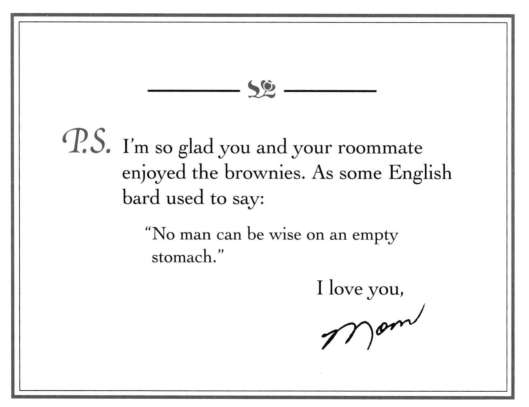

P.S. I'm so glad you and your roommate
enjoyed the brownies. As some English
bard used to say:

"No man can be wise on an empty
stomach."

I love you,

Mom

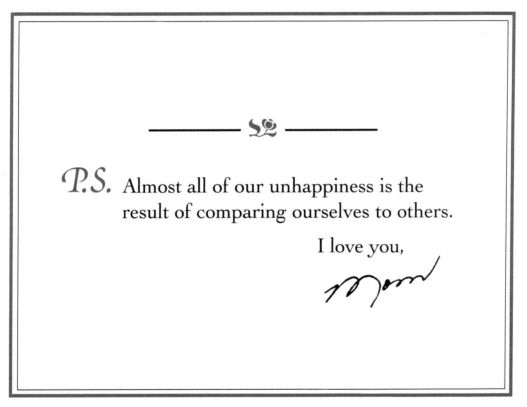

P.S. Almost all of our unhappiness is the result of comparing ourselves to others.

I love you,

Mom

P.S. Someone wrote:

"A spade and a kind word should
never be allowed to rust."

That reminds me of your grandfather's
advice to compliment at least three
people every day.

I love you,

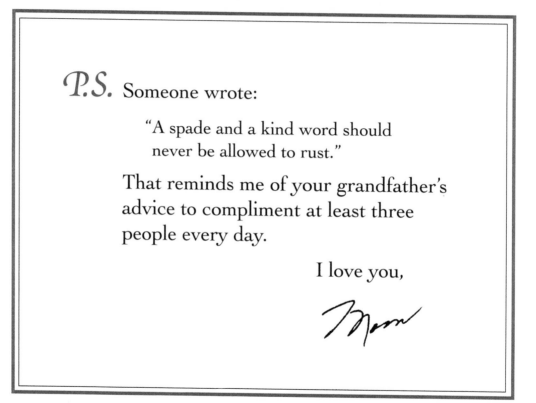

P.S. Sometimes your father has a tendency to boast just a little bit—especially around old friends. I left this note in his sock drawer:

> Don't brag. It's not the whistle that moves the train.

Think he got the message?

I love you,

Mom

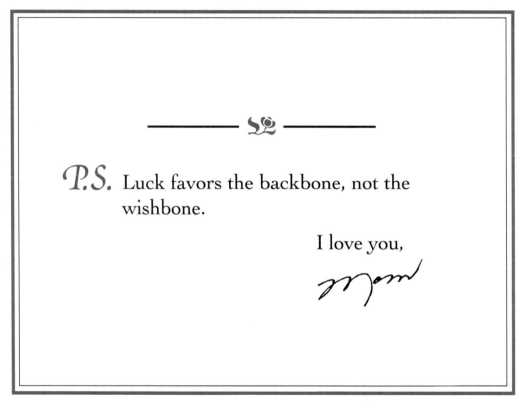

P.S. Luck favors the backbone, not the wishbone.

I love you,

Mom

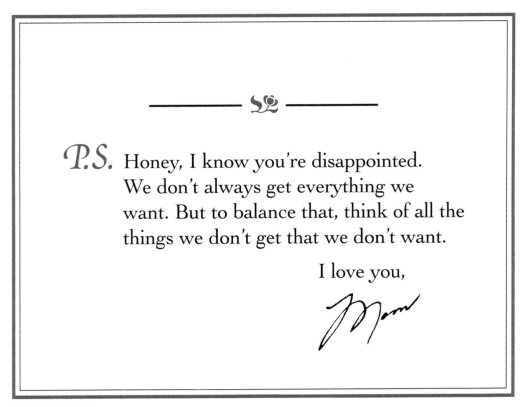

P.S. Honey, I know you're disappointed. We don't always get everything we want. But to balance that, think of all the things we don't get that we don't want.

I love you,

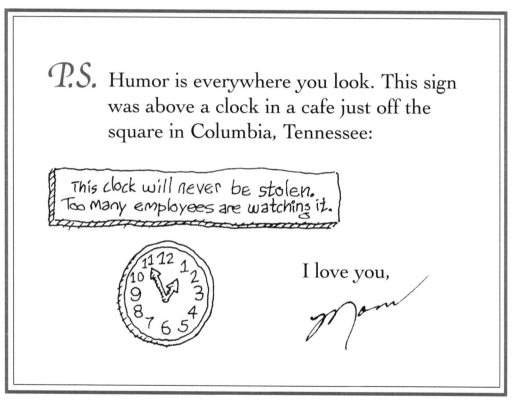

P.S. Humor is everywhere you look. This sign was above a clock in a cafe just off the square in Columbia, Tennessee:

> This clock will never be stolen.
> Too many employees are watching it.

I love you,

Mom

P.S. Every day we are given stones. But what do we build? Is it a bridge or is it a wall?

I love you,

Mom

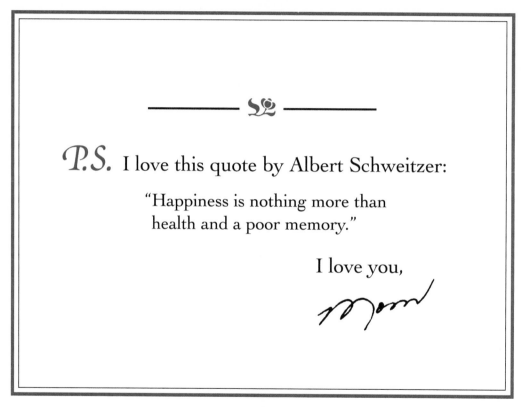

P.S. I love this quote by Albert Schweitzer:

"Happiness is nothing more than
health and a poor memory."

I love you,

Mom

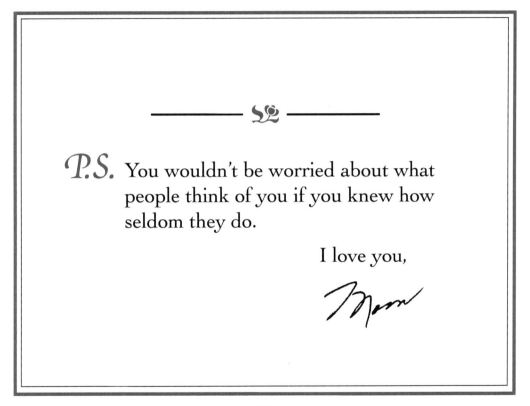

P.S. You wouldn't be worried about what people think of you if you knew how seldom they do.

I love you,

Mom

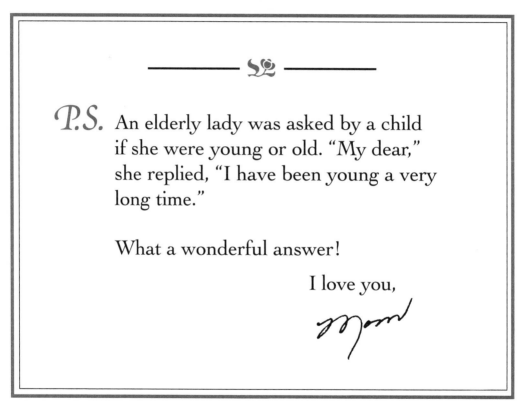

P.S. An elderly lady was asked by a child if she were young or old. "My dear," she replied, "I have been young a very long time."

What a wonderful answer!

I love you,

Mom

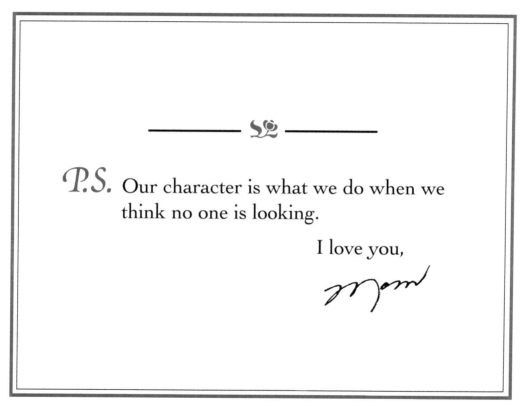

P.S. Our character is what we do when we think no one is looking.

I love you,

Mom

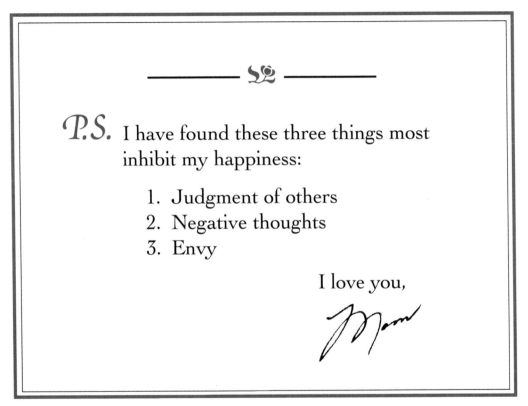

P.S. I have found these three things most inhibit my happiness:

1. Judgment of others
2. Negative thoughts
3. Envy

I love you,

Mom

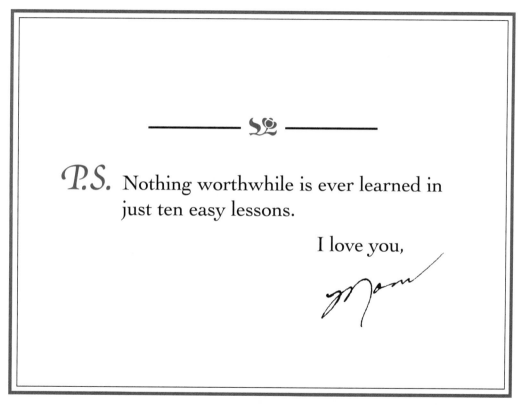

P.S. Nothing worthwhile is ever learned in just ten easy lessons.

I love you,

Mom

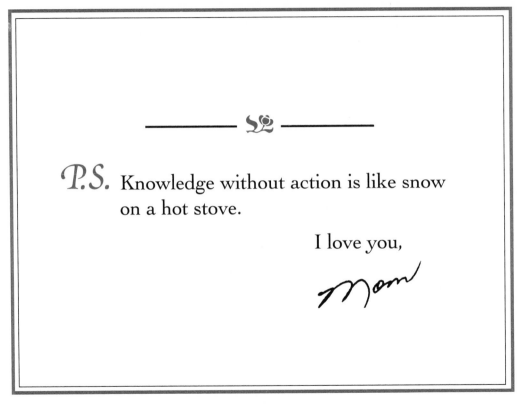

P.S. Knowledge without action is like snow on a hot stove.

I love you,

Mom

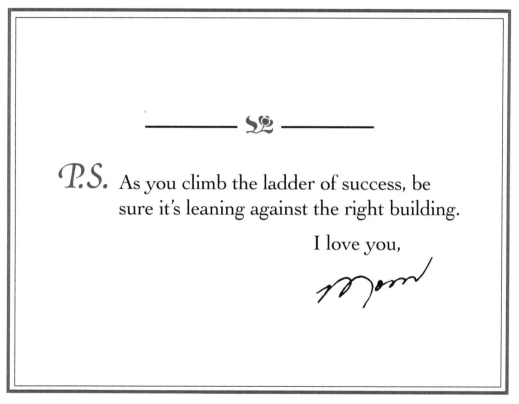

P.S. As you climb the ladder of success, be
sure it's leaning against the right building.

I love you,

Mom

P.S. Last night we visited Uncle Wallace in the hospital. As we were leaving, I saw a hand-lettered sign above a patient's bed. It read,

> I have cancer
> But cancer doesn't have me.

Imagine the courage and character of the patient. I was so touched and inspired. I've thought about it all day.

I love you,

Mom

P.S. John Luther wrote this about character:

> "Good character is more to be praised than outstanding talent. Most talents are, to some extent, a gift. Good character, by contrast, is not given to us. We have to build it piece by piece—by thought, choice, courage, and determination."

I'm so proud of your fine character.

I love you,

Mom

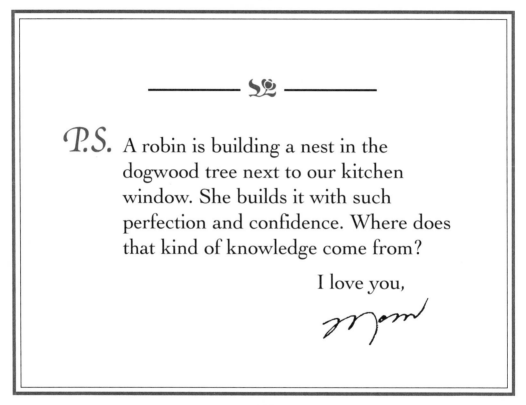

P.S. A robin is building a nest in the
dogwood tree next to our kitchen
window. She builds it with such
perfection and confidence. Where does
that kind of knowledge come from?

I love you,

Mom

———— 💮 ————

P.S. Luck is what happens when preparation
meets opportunity.

I love you,

Mom

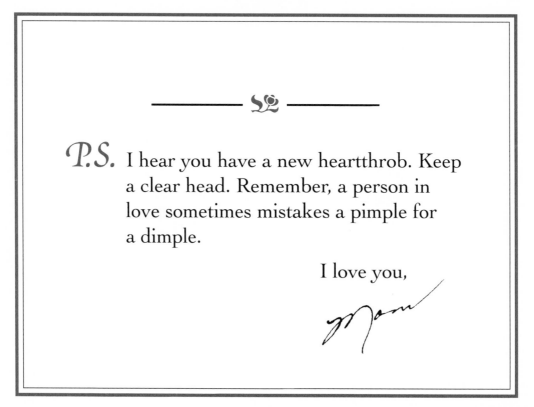

P.S. I hear you have a new heartthrob. Keep a clear head. Remember, a person in love sometimes mistakes a pimple for a dimple.

I love you,

Mom

P.S. I couldn't help but smile when I saw this bumper sticker on the back of an old pickup truck parked at Wal-Mart:

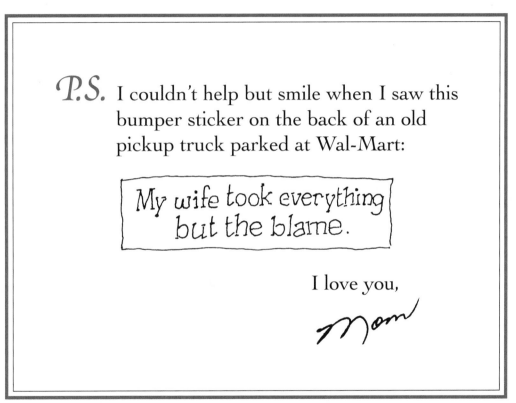

My wife took everything but the blame.

I love you,

Mom

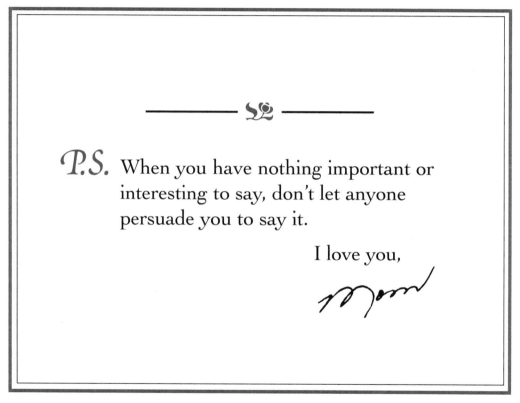

P.S. When you have nothing important or interesting to say, don't let anyone persuade you to say it.

I love you,

Mom

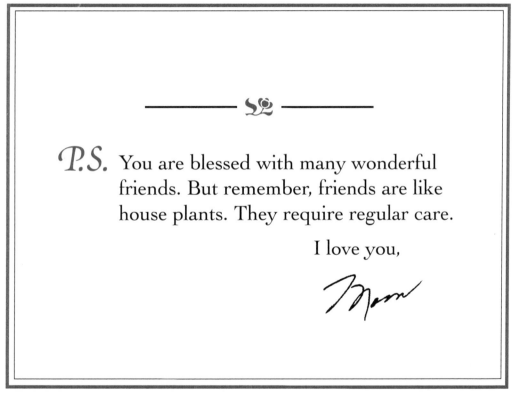

P.S. You are blessed with many wonderful friends. But remember, friends are like house plants. They require regular care.

I love you,

Mom

P.S. Job interviews are tiresome and stressful, but they can also be enlightening. With your talent, intelligence, and enthusiasm, I know you'll soon find the perfect job. I remember someone telling me long ago, "Find a job you like and you add five days to every week."

I love you,

Mom

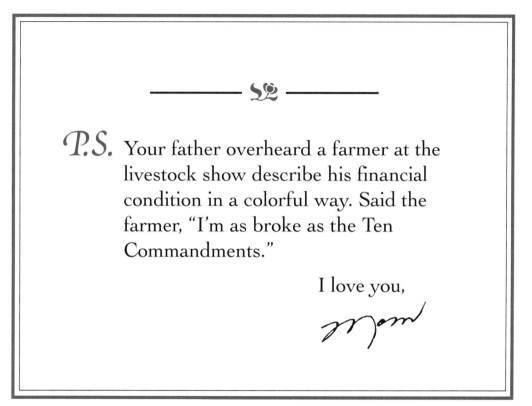

P.S. Your father overheard a farmer at the livestock show describe his financial condition in a colorful way. Said the farmer, "I'm as broke as the Ten Commandments."

I love you,

Mom

P.S. Margaret has this framed and hanging in her kitchen:

Bon appetit!

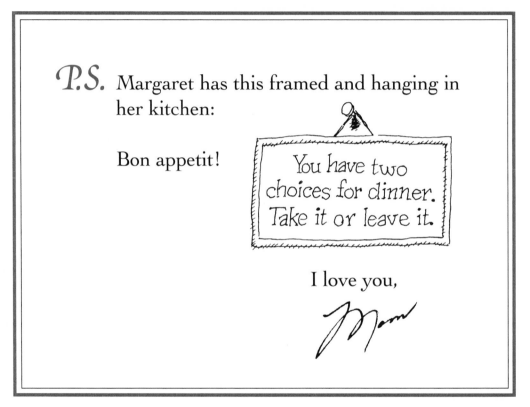

You have two choices for dinner. Take it or leave it.

I love you,

Mom

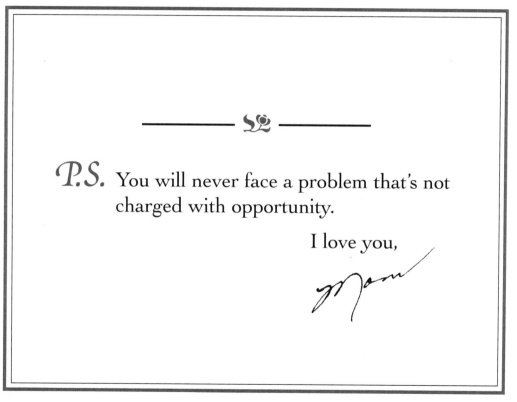

P.S. You will never face a problem that's not charged with opportunity.

I love you,

Mom

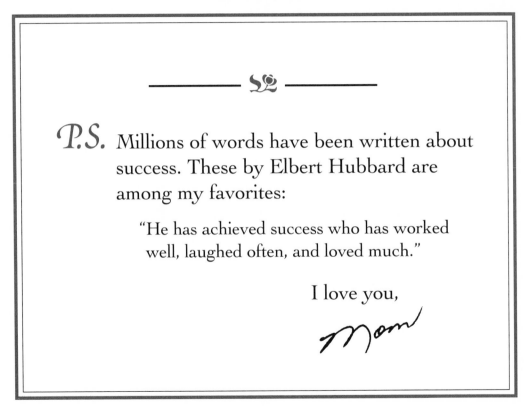

P.S. Millions of words have been written about success. These by Elbert Hubbard are among my favorites:

"He has achieved success who has worked well, laughed often, and loved much."

I love you,

Mom

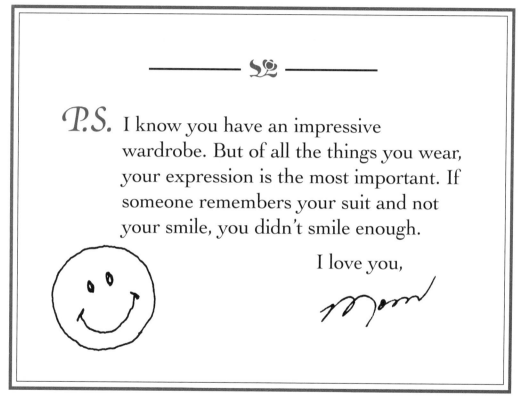

P.S. I know you have an impressive wardrobe. But of all the things you wear, your expression is the most important. If someone remembers your suit and not your smile, you didn't smile enough.

I love you,

Mom

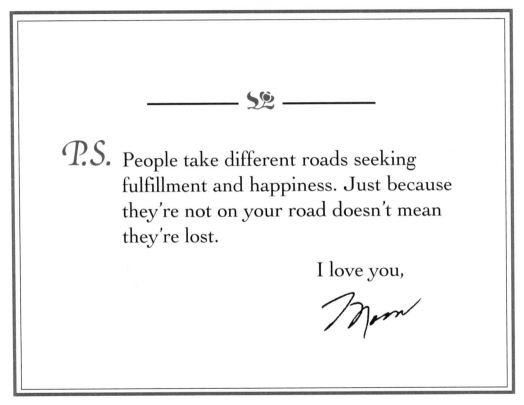

P.S. People take different roads seeking fulfillment and happiness. Just because they're not on your road doesn't mean they're lost.

I love you,

Mom

———— ❧ ————

P.S. Last night your father and I reviewed our retirement savings. We've decided we have enough to last us the rest of our lives—unless we decide to buy something!

Oh, well.

I love you,

Mom

P.S. Everyone from time to time needs a
little boost. If you ever see a turtle on a
fence post, remember he had some help
getting there.

I love you,

Mom

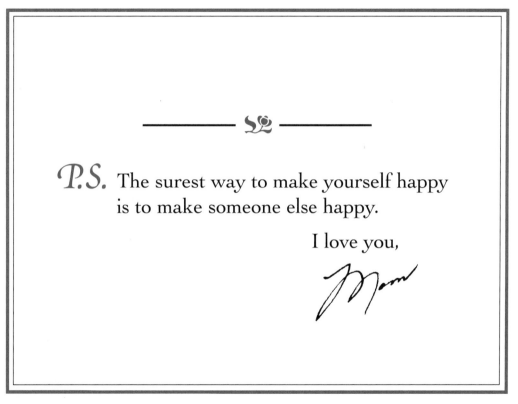

P.S. The surest way to make yourself happy
is to make someone else happy.

I love you,

Mom

P.S. One of God's greatest miracles is to enable ordinary people to do extraordinary things.

I love you,

Mom

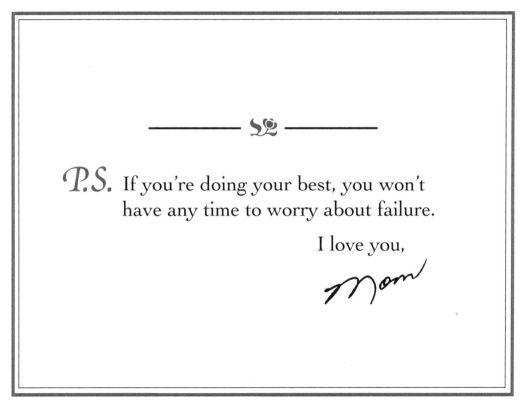

P.S. If you're doing your best, you won't have any time to worry about failure.

I love you,

Mom

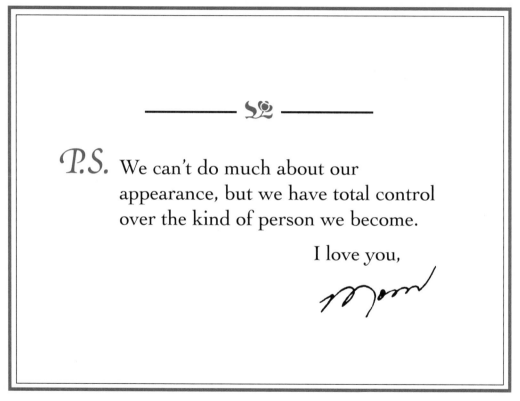

P.S. We can't do much about our appearance, but we have total control over the kind of person we become.

I love you,

Mom

P.S. I know you're angry with Alec. Why not try this. Write him a letter. Pour out all of your feelings—describe your anger and disappointment. Don't hold anything back. Then put the letter in a drawer. After two days take it out and read it. Do you still want to send it? I've found that anger and pie crusts soften after two days.

I love you,

Mom

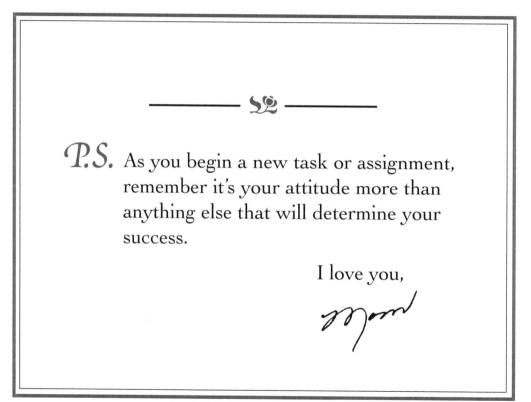

P.S. As you begin a new task or assignment, remember it's your attitude more than anything else that will determine your success.

I love you,

Mom

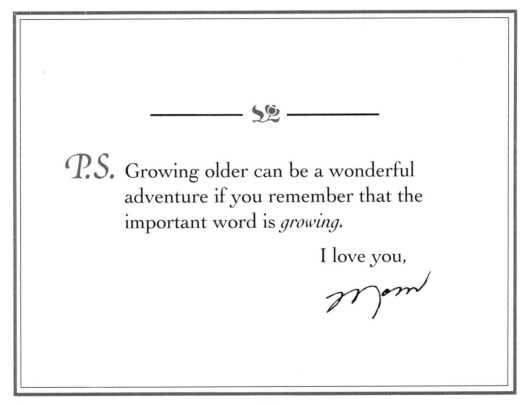

P.S. Growing older can be a wonderful
adventure if you remember that the
important word is *growing*.

I love you,

Mom

P.S. Here's challenging advice from Og Mandino, the famous writer and speaker:

> "Beginning today, treat everyone you meet as if they were going to be dead by midnight. Extend to them all the care, kindness, and understanding you can muster, and do it with no thought of any reward. Your life will never be the same again."

I love you,

Mom

P.S. So you wish that all the problems at work would go away. Maybe you'd better think again. When problems cease, so do opportunities. Solving problems was the reason you were hired. And it's been my experience that jobs with few problems don't pay very much.

I love you,

Mom

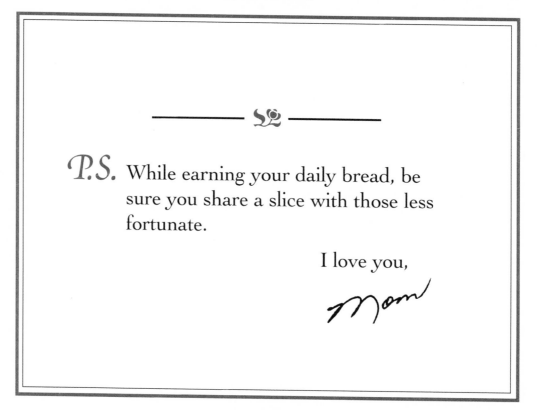

P.S. While earning your daily bread, be sure you share a slice with those less fortunate.

I love you,

Mom

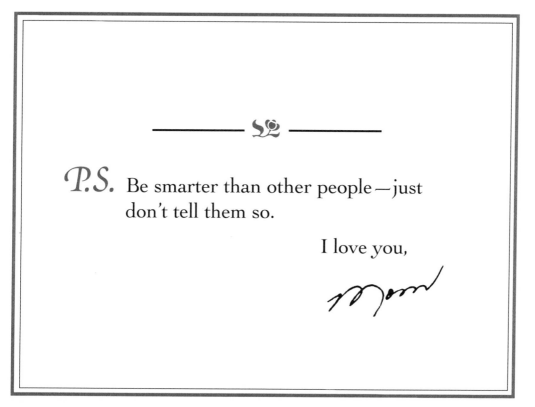

P.S. Be smarter than other people—just don't tell them so.

I love you,

Mom

P.S. Love is like wildflowers. It's often found in the most unlikely places.

I love you,

Mom

———— 🌹 ————

P.S. Remember the Golden Rule. And remember it's your turn.

I love you,

Mom

P.S. I don't know the author of the following, but it is inspiring:

> "The people on our planet are not standing in a line single file. Look closely. Everyone is really standing in a circle, holding hands. Whatever you give to the person standing next to you, it eventually comes back to you."

Beautiful.

I love you,

Mom